EARLY PEOPLES

CHINESE OF THE SHANG, ZHOU, AND QIN DYNASTIES

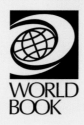

WORLD
BOOK

World Book
a Scott Fetzer company
Chicago
www.worldbookonline.com

World Book, Inc.
233 N. Michigan Avenue
Chicago, IL 60601
U.S.A.

For information about other World Book publications, visit our
Web site at http://www.worldbookonline.com or call
1-800-WORLDBK (967-5325).
For information about sales to schools and libraries, call
1-800-975-3250 (United States), or 1-800-837-5365 (Canada).

Library of Congress Cataloging-in-Publication Data

Chinese of the Shang, Zhou, and Qin dynasties.
    p. cm. -- (Early peoples)
  Includes index.
  Summary: "A discussion of early Chinese peoples of the
Shang, Zhou, and Qin dynasties, including who they were,
where they lived, the rise of civilization, social structure,
religion, art and architecture, science and technology, daily
life, entertainment and sports, and fall of civilization.
Features include timelines, fact boxes, glossary, list of
recommended reading and Web sites"--Provided by publisher.
  ISBN 978-0-7166-2141-6
  1. China--History--Shang dynasty, 1766-1122 B.C.--Juvenile
literature. 2. China--History--Zhou dynasty, 1122-221 B.C.--
Juvenile literature. 3. China---History--Qin dynasty, 221-207
B.C.--Juvenile literature. I. World Book, Inc.
  DS744C3875 2009
  931--dc22
                                    2008028058

Printed in China by Leo Paper Products Ltd.,
Heshan, Guangdong
2nd printing June 2010

STAFF

EXECUTIVE COMMITTEE
President
  Paul A. Gazzolo
Vice President and Chief Marketing Officer
  Patricia Ginnis
Vice President and Chief Financial Officer
  Donald D. Keller
Vice President and Editor in Chief
  Paul A. Kobasa
Director, Human Resources
  Bev Ecker
Chief Technology Officer
  Tim Hardy
Managing Director, International
  Benjamin Hinton

EDITORIAL
Editor in Chief
  Paul A. Kobasa
Associate Director, Supplementary
Publications
  Scott Thomas
Managing Editor, Supplementary
Publications
  Barbara A. Mayes
Senior Editor, Supplementary Publications
  Kristina Vaicikonis
Manager, Research, Supplementary
Publications
  Cheryl Graham
Manager, Contracts & Compliance
  (Rights & Permissions)
  Loranne K. Shields

Administrative Assistant
  Ethel Matthews
Editors
  Nicholas Kilzer
  Scott Richardson
  Christine Sullivan

GRAPHICS AND DESIGN
Associate Director
  Sandra M. Dyrlund
Manager
  Tom Evans
Coordinator, Design Development and
Production
  Brenda B. Tropinski

EDITORIAL ADMINISTRATION
Director, Systems and Projects
  Tony Tills
Senior Manager, Publishing Operations
  Timothy Falk

PRODUCTION
Director, Manufacturing and Pre-Press
  Carma Fazio
Manufacturing Manager
  Steve Hueppchen
Production/Technology Manager
  Anne Fritzinger
Production Specialist
  Curley Hunter
Proofreader
  Emilie Schrage

MARKETING
Chief Marketing Officer
  Patricia Ginnis
Associate Director, School and Library
Marketing
  Jennifer Parello

Produced for World Book by
  White-Thomson Publishing Ltd.
  +44 (0) 845 362 8240
  www.wtpub.co.uk
Steve White-Thomson, President

Writer: Alan Wachtel
Editors: Valerie Weber, Robert Famighetti
Designer: Simon Borrough
Photo Researcher: Amy Sparks
Map Artist: Stefan Chabluk
Illustrator: Adam Hook (p. 24)
Fact Checker: Charlene Rimsa
Proofreader: Catherine Gardner
Indexer: Nila Glikin

Consultant:
David D. Buck
Emeritus Professor of History
University of Wisconsin-Milwaukee

TABLE OF CONTENTS

Glossary There is a glossary on pages 60-61. Terms defined in the glossary are in type **that looks like this** on their first appearance on any spread (two facing pages).

Additional Resources Books for further reading and recommended Web sites are listed on page 62. Because of the nature of the Internet, some Web site addresses may have changed since publication. The publisher has no responsibility for any such changes or for the content of cited sources.

WHO WERE THE SHANG, ZHOU, AND QIN?

The Shang *(shahng)*, Zhou *(joh)*, and Qin *(chihn)* were all ruling families, or **dynasties** *(DY nuh steez)*, of China. For much of its history, China was ruled by dynasties. These dynasties were so powerful that entire periods of China's history are named after them.

The Shang

The Shang dynasty was one of China's earliest. Shang rule began in about 1766 B.C. and ended in 1045 B.C. The Shang ruled over a small section of the land that is modern China.

The Zhou

The Zhou, also spelled Chou, was another powerful family. The Zhou took over from the Shang when that dynasty weakened. The Zhou dynasty lasted from 1045 B.C. until 256 B.C. Like the Shang, the Zhou ruled over only a section of what is now modern China.

▼ From the Shang through the Qin, each of ancient China's successive dynasties ruled a larger territory than the dynasty before it. Still, these territories were much smaller than the present-day country of China.

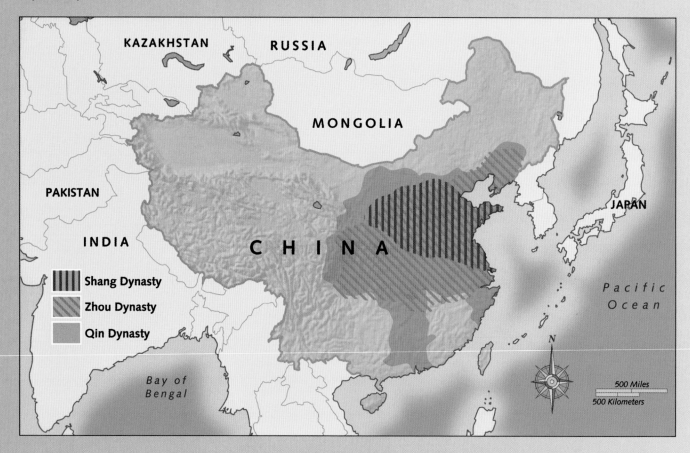

◄ One of the most famous and impressive structures ever built, the Great Wall winds through northern China. The wall's total length is about 4,500 miles (7,240 kilometers). Shi Huangdi *(shihr hwahng dee),* the emperor from the Qin dynasty who unified ancient China, began the Great Wall in the 200's B.C. by connecting new walls with smaller, older walls that had already been built.

The Qin

From 256 B.C. to 221 B.C., seven large states struggled for control of China. Finally, in 221 B.C., the Qin, sometimes spelled Ch'in, dynasty gained control. This dynasty ruled until 206 B.C.—only about 15 years. However, the Qin dynasty was the first to unify ancient China into a single nation. While the area ruled by the Qin was smaller in area than modern China is today, it was considerably larger than the lands ruled by the Shang or Zhou.

Changing Times

The Shang, Zhou, and Qin dynasties together lasted more than 1,500 years. There is much we do not know about peoples' lives during this period. The first written records from China that have been discovered date to about 1500 B.C., about 250 years after the start of the Shang dynasty. The first written history of China dates to about 100 B.C. What we do know about the period reveals a lively and changing time of developing **culture,** government, and technology. Historians and **archaeologists** *(AHR kee OL uh jihstz)* have given us new knowledge about this interesting time in China's past.

TIMELINE OF ANCIENT CHINA

about 1766 B.C.
The Shang dynasty begins.

1500 B.C.
Earliest known writing in China is dated to this time.

about 1250 B.C.
Tomb of Lady Fu Hao *(foo how)* is built.

1045 B.C.
The Zhou dynasty begins.

about 700 B.C.
Iron is used in China.

770 B.C. to 475 B.C
Spring and Autumn Period.

475 B.C. to 221 B.C.
Warring States Period.

200's B.C.
Early building on Great Wall is traditionally dated to this time.

221 B.C. to 206 B.C.
The Qin dynasty rules.

206 B.C.
The Han dynasty begins.

WHERE DID THE SHANG, ZHOU, AND QIN RULE?

The area ruled by the Shang, Zhou, and Qin **dynasties** covered most of the Loess *(LOH ihs)* Plateau, which includes the North China Plain. The major **archaeological sites** of ancient China are located in this area. Archaeological sites are places where remains of past human **cultures** have been found. Ancient China occupied mainly the modern Chinese **provinces** *(PROV uhns ehz)* of Shanxi *(shahn shee)*, Shandong *(shahn duhng)*, and Henan *(huh nahn)*. This area is only a portion of the huge modern nation of China. To the ancient Chinese people, however, this land was the whole world. By around 1000 B.C., they called it tianxia *(tyen shyah)*, or "All-Under-Heaven."

Climate and Geography of the Region

The land of ancient China's dynasties had two main geographical regions, the North and the South. The main features of the northern region are the Yellow River and the Loess Plateau. Loess is a type of soil that is dry and crumbly. The northern region of China is fairly cold and dry. It does not get much rainfall—in some parts, fewer than 20 inches (50 centimeters) per year.

▼ One of the Three Gorges (deep, narrow valleys) of China's Yangtze River. Many wars were fought in the region of the Three Gorges during the Shang, Zhou, and Qin dynasties. In recent years, the Chinese government's construction of the Three Gorges Dam across the Yangtze has created a huge reservoir that extends for hundreds of miles behind the dam, putting under water a number of archaeological sites.

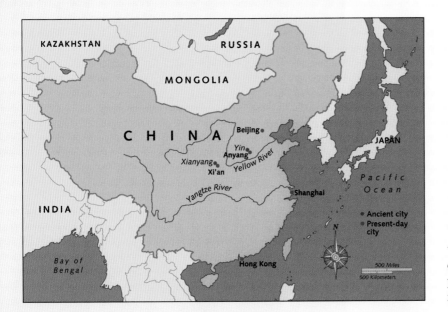

◀ A map of some of the ancient capitals of the Shang and Qin dynasties, as well as present-day cities and two of China's major rivers.

Compared with the northern region, China's southern region is much warmer and wetter. It gets an average of about 60 inches (150 centimeters) of rain per year. In much of this region, the plants and trees are always green. The southern region features the Yangtze *(yahng dzuh)* River and many smaller rivers.

Moving Capitals

Both the Shang and Zhou dynasties had different capitals during different time periods. During the Shang dynasty, there was an area called Central Shang. Central Shang was located in the northern part of the modern province of Henan. The last Shang capital, Yin *(yin)* was also in Central Shang, near the modern-day city of Anyang *(ahn yahng)*. The Zhou dynasty may have had capitals at Feng *(fuhng)* and Hao *(how)*, but these cities have never been found.

The founder of the Qin dynasty, Shi Huangdi (also spelled Shih Huang-ti), took control after a period of warfare among Zhou states. Shi Huangdi founded a new capital at Xianyang *(shee ehn yuhng)*, which is near today's city of Xi'an *(shee ahn)*. Shi Huangdi's family name— Qin *(chin)*—was the source of the western word *China*.

DISCOVERING YIN

Archaeologists decided to explore and **excavate** at the Shang capital of Yin in 1928. They knew that antique dealers had found **artifacts** *(AHR tuh faktz)*— objects made by people in the past— from this area. Archaeologists were amazed at what they discovered. In addition to artifacts, they found building foundations and burial sites. One such burial site, discovered in 1976, was the tomb of Lady Fu Hao, whom archaeologists believe to have died in about 1250 B.C. Fu Hao was the wife of a Shang king. The items in her tomb included **vessels**, some of which were shaped like animals; objects carved from **jade**; pottery; and cowrie *(KOW ree)* shells, which served as money at the time. Dogs and humans had been sacrificed and were buried in the tomb with Lady Fu Hao. Later dynasties would bury **terra-cotta** *(TEHR uh KOT uh)* figures with the dead in place of sacrificed humans.

Achievements of the Shang, Zhou, and Qin Dynasties

The period of the Shang, Zhou, and Qin **dynasties** was a time of great cultural, artistic, and technological achievement.

Shang

The most important achievement of the Shang dynasty was the development of a system of writing. This occurred sometime before 1500 B.C., the date of the first known record. The Shang writing system, which was based on **pictograms** *(PIHK tuh gramz)*, provided the foundation for modern Chinese writing.

Craftsmen of the Shang dynasty also became highly skilled in the working of **bronze,** a mixture made primarily of copper and tin. Many of the **artifacts** that survive from the Shang dynasty are **vessels**—that is, cups, bowls, and pots—fashioned in bronze.

The Shang dynasty is also known for the development of elaborate **rituals** for the worship of their gods and ancestors. The rituals most commonly involved appealing to the gods and ancestors for help with hunting, farming, and building. The king played the central role in these rituals. **Diviners** *(duh VY nuhrz)*, people who foretold the future, also played a role.

Zhou

Like the Shang dynasty, the Zhou dynasty is known for its beautiful bronze work. However, China underwent an **Iron Age** during the Zhou dynasty that began around 700 B.C. After this time, the Chinese made many weapons and farming tools out of iron.

▼ A bronze ritual vase with elaborate decoration from the late Shang or early Zhou dynasty. Both dynasties are known for their skills in the crafting of bronze.

Religious **rituals,** arts, and writing continued to develop during the Zhou dynasty. The oldest known book of Chinese poetry—a collection of 305 poems called *The Book of Songs*—and other classic works of Chinese writing were completed during this era.

The Zhou dynasty leaders set up a system of rule that was similar to the **feudal** *(FYOO duhl)* system that developed in Europe during the Middle Ages (A.D. 400's-1400's). Under a feudal system, a king gives land to lords. In return, the lords swear allegiance to the king, particularly during times of war. Although the lords ruled over the land given them, they ranked beneath the king in power and importance. The Chinese word for this system is Fengjian *(fuhng jehn)*.

Qin

Although the Qin dynasty lasted a very short time—only about 15 years—its greatest achievement is China's greatest landmark, the Great Wall. Different Chinese states had begun building walls in the second half of the Zhou dynasty. The Qin dynasty linked all these walls and added thousands of more miles of wall, creating the longest structure on Earth.

The Qin dynasty is also known for the tomb of its founder and the first emperor of China, Shi Huangdi. The tomb contained the famous **terra-cotta** army, more than 6,000 life-sized, terra-cotta statues of soldiers, horses, chariots, and other figures. The army, discovered in 1974, is one of the greatest archaeological finds of all time.

EARLY CHINESE WRITING

Shang writing is based on pictures. These pictures are called pictograms, or pictographs. Instead of using letters from an alphabet to make up words, Shang writing used pictograms to stand for people, places, things, and actions. The Shang linked these pictograms together to make sentences. Scientists have discovered the meanings of more than 1,000 Shang pictograms. Most of the writing we have from the Shang is on **oracle bones** *(AWR uh kuhl bonz)*, animal bones with markings or writing on them. The bones were used to ask questions of the gods and ancestors and record what was believed to be their answers.

▶ A Shang dynasty oracle bone found in Anyang. The oldest Chinese writing is the engraved characters found on oracle bones.

ORIGINS OF THE SHANG

Primitive humans lived in the area that is now China more than 1 million years ago. By 100,000 B.C., *Homo sapiens (HOH moh SAY pee uhnz)*, or modern humans, inhabited the region.

Ancestors of the Ancient Chinese

Beginning in about 5000 B.C., the people of this region created a **culture** that was different from the cultures of other early humans. These ancestors of the ancient Chinese developed crafts and their own religion and practices for burying the dead. **Archaeologists** have discovered a number of **artifacts** made by these Chinese ancestors, including many pieces of well-formed pottery. The people of this culture also carved objects out of **jade** and made some weapons out of metal.

▶ A pottery vase from the ancient Yangshao *(yahng show)* culture. This culture existed from 5000 to 3000 B.C., before the earliest Chinese dynasties.

By around 3000 B.C., different groups in ancient China came to be led by powerful chiefs. These groups built settlements surrounded by huge walls. One of these walls stood about 20 feet (6 meters) high and 29 feet (8.8 meters) thick!

From studying objects found in graves, archaeologists have concluded that this society had a number of different classes. The graves of certain people were filled with valuable objects, an indication of high status *(STAT uhs)*, or a high place in a society. Other graves contained no objects, not even evidence that the remains had been buried in a coffin.

▶ A three-legged wine **vessel** that is the earliest known decorated Chinese **bronze**. It dates back to about 2000 B.C. and is from the Xia dynasty, the dynasty immediately before the Shang.

坑儒焚坑儒焚

PROOF OF THE XIA DYNASTY

For a long time, historians had no real evidence that the Xia dynasty had ever existed, and many thought it was simply a legend. However, in 1959, archaeologists digging at Erlitou *(uhr lee toh)*, located in the **province** of Henan, found remains of building foundations that dated to 1900 B.C. This included the foundations for buildings that seem to have been palaces. Finding remains of a culture that existed before the Shang was the first evidence that there had been an earlier dynasty.

The Xia Dynasty

The oldest known ancient Chinese history book— *Shi Ji (shuh tsee)*, or *Records of the Historian* or *The Historical Records*—was written in about 100 B.C. It relates a **legend** of Yu *(yoo)*, a leader who saved many people from floods. The book records that Yu was the first leader of a **dynasty** called the Xia *(shyah)*. The Xia ruled from about 2100 B.C. to 1766 B.C., before the Shang. *Shi Ji* is also an account of other Xia leaders, capitals, and history.

ANCIENT CHINESE CIVILIZATION AT ITS HEIGHT

▲ The extent of the land ruled, in turn, by the Shang, Zhou, and Qin dynasties.

Each of the three **dynasties**, the Shang, Zhou, and Qin, occupied the same core area. And each enlarged that area until the Qin lands stretched north nearly to present-day Mongolia and North Korea and south to the South China Sea.

Extent of Shang Rule

No one knows exactly how much land the Shang dynasty controlled. Historians believe that most of the people who supported the Shang government lived in areas that are now part of the **provinces** of Henan and Shanxi in modern China. Although the Shang dynasty may have controlled only a small area, the influence of Shang religion and crafts was

A NEW SYSTEM OF GOVERNMENT

The feudal system ended with the Qin. Under the Qin's new system, the area ruled by the emperor was divided into districts. Each district was ruled by a governor, who was appointed by the emperor. At the same time, the aristocratic families that had ruled lost their power. Many of these families were made to move from the lands they had ruled to the capital of the Qin **empire** at Xianyang. Many features of the system of government that began under the Qin were still in place when the last emperor of China, Pu Yi *(poo yee)*, lost his throne in 1912.

widespread. More than 14 of China's 22 provinces have **archaeological sites** that contain Shang **artifacts** and display evidence of the Shang **culture.**

Extent of Zhou Rule

The original kingdom of Zhou lay west of the Shang capital, Yin. The Zhou state was already powerful during the Shang dynasty. As the Shang dynasty weakened, the Zhou grew in power. After making **alliances** *(uh LY uhns ehz)* with other peoples, the Zhou attacked the Shang and conquered them. Gradually, the Zhou took over the whole Yellow River plain region.

Zhou kings sent members of their family to set up fortresses and rule new territories in the conquered lands. They also made local rulers into **feudal** lords who ruled for them. By the 700's B.C., there were about 200 Zhou lords. The Zhou kings, however, always retained their power. The Zhou central government had a royal army, which fought with the lords' troops against shared enemies. The royal army also ensured that the lords' armies remained loyal to the Zhou kings.

Extent of Qin Rule

The Zhou feudal system slowly lost power, and from 770 B.C. until 221 B.C., there were many wars. At first, the land of the Qin was within Zhou territory. The Qin's power grew during a time known as the Warring States Period, which lasted from 475 B.C. to 221 B.C. By the end of this period, the Qin had conquered all the land that was ruled by the Zhou. The Qin had also conquered territories to the west and the south of the area that had been once ruled by the Zhou. With this, the Qin unified a number of different groups under one ruler.

◀ An intricately carved **jade** pendant made around the time of the late Zhou dynasty. The pendant is shaped like a phoenix *(FEE nihks)*, a mythical bird.

THE GREAT WALL

The longest structure ever built on Earth, the Great Wall is perhaps the most famous landmark in China. It stretches about 5,500 miles (8,850 kilometers) across northern China, including about 3,890 miles (6,260 kilometers) of handmade walls as well as such natural barriers as rivers and hills. The Great Wall extends from the Bo Gulf of the Yellow Sea to the Jiayu Pass in what is now Gansu province in western China.

Making Connections

In 221 B.C., Shi Huangdi of the Qin **dynasty** unified China and became the first emperor. By this time, hundreds of miles of wall had already been built. Attacks from the north, however, were still a problem. Shi Huangdi responded by connecting parts of the walls belonging to different areas and adding thousands of miles of new wall. The Great Wall—and the armies stationed along it—did not just defend the **empire** from attack. They also symbolized the first emperor's great power.

The Great Wall winds over green hills, craggy mountains, and dusty hillsides. Builders used the materials that were found near the section that they were building. In the mountains,

▼ The Great Wall represents an amazing achievement of engineering. Sections of the wall have been rebuilt over the centuries, and new sections have been added.

▲ The Jiayuguan *(jah yoo geh wahn)* Fortress stands at the western end of the Great Wall. This fortress was built during the Ming dynasty.

A Matter of Myths

It is often reported that astronauts can see the Great Wall of China from space. This is not really true. Even when in a low orbit above Earth, astronauts cannot spot the Great Wall unaided. In fact, even in detailed photos taken by astronauts in space, it is very difficult to see the Great Wall, especially because the material that the wall was made from is similar to the surrounding land.

the wall was made up of stone. On the plains, workers built with rammed earth, a type of construction whereby soil is placed into a form and is then pounded and compressed.

The Wall After the Qin Dynasty

After the Qin dynasty fell, the Han dynasty (206 B.C. to A.D. 220) took over. Wall building continued during the Han and for more than a thousand years after that dynasty's end. During this time, much of the Qin wall fell and was replaced. Most of what we see today of the Great Wall of China was built in the A.D. 1400's under the Ming *(mihng)* dynasty, which ruled from 1368 to 1644. The Ming also added watchtowers, fortresses, and cannons to the wall.

LEADERS OF ANCIENT CHINA

The Shang, Zhou, and Qin **dynasties** all went through periods when the power of the rulers grew and shrank, depending on conditions and on individual abilities.

Thirty Shang Kings

The Shang dynasty is thought to have had a series of 30 kings. The position of king passed from father to son or sometimes from brother to brother. Although the names of the Shang kings are listed in the ancient book called the *Shi Ji*, for a long time there was no proof that these kings existed. In the 1800's, people found animal bones buried around the location of the ancient city of Yin. The bones were sold as "dragon bones" in the markets and used as medicines. Eventually, in 1899, scholars recognized the carvings on the bones as ancient writings. Then, **archaeologists** began **excavating** the Shang city of Yin and found thousands of **oracle bones** from Shang times. Names written on these oracle bones matched the names given in the *Shi Ji* for the Shang kings. This discovery led scholars to believe the names in the *Shi Ji* referred to kings who had actually lived and provided the scholars with information about Shang kings who had lived thousands of years before.

◄ Shi Huangdi, in a painting from the A.D. 1700's, was the powerful Qin dynasty leader who unified China and is considered the first emperor. The painting is from a set of portraits of Chinese emperors that is now part of the collection of the British Library, the national library of the United Kingdom.

Ritual Leaders

One of the main roles of Shang kings was to lead **rituals.** Some of these rituals required the sacrifice of people or animals. The Shang believed that the king had a special connection to ancestors, who could in turn speak to the gods. It was this special connection to ancestors that made the king worthy to rule. In addition to being ritual leaders, Shang kings were also government leaders.

The Zhou Dynasty

The Zhou dynasty remained strong for many years. Historians divide the time of the Zhou dynasty into two main divisions. The first half is called the Western Zhou. It lasted from 1045 B.C. to 770 B.C. The second half is itself divided into two periods: the Spring and Autumn Period—which lasted from 770 B.C. to 475 B.C.—and the Warring States Period—which ran from 475 B.C. to 221 B.C. The Spring and Autumn and Warring States periods weakened the Zhou, and they lost power to **feudal** lords. Left vulnerable by this weakness, the Zhou dynasty fell to Shi Huangdi, the powerful general who established the Qin dynasty in 221 B.C.

The Qin and Shi Huangdi

As the person who imposed the first single government across China, Shi Huangdi is considered the first emperor of China. He is known for the huge construction projects carried out during his reign. He built many roads in addition to an important section of the Great Wall. Shi Huangdi's armies could move easily around the country on the roads, and the Great Wall kept out his enemies.

▲ The Zhou ruler Mu Wang *(moo wahng),* who lived from about 985 B.C. to 907 B.C., travels grandly in a horse-drawn chariot in a painting from the A.D. 1600's. The picture, painted on silk, was based on details from a history of Chinese emperors.

WHAT WERE ORACLE BONES?

Most of the oracle bones from the Shang period are made of the shoulder blades of oxen or the shells of turtles. The **diviner** would carve a question onto the bone. Then a piece of hot metal would be placed on the bone, causing it to crack. The diviner would interpret these cracks to provide an answer to the question. The answer that had been provided and other information would then be carved into the bone.

THE UPPER CLASSES

Society in ancient China was made up of people of different classes. Directly below the rulers of the Shang, Zhou, and Qin **dynasties** stood a class of **aristocrats**.

GIFTS FOR THE KINGS

Shang aristocrats sent tributes to the king. Different states and leaders sent humans, often prisoners of war, who were usually sacrificed in **rituals** for ancestor worship. Animals, such as cattle or white horses, were also given. The donation of large numbers of turtle shells and cattle shoulder blades to be used as **oracle bones** helped with the many **divinations** during the Shang dynasty.

◀ The powerful Qin emperor Shi Huangdi is shown in a painting from the A.D. 1600's, painted on silk. The emperor is surrounded by lords and is carried in a kind of sedan chair by servants.

Shang Aristocrats

The aristocrat class was one of the great strengths of the Shang dynasty. The local lords provided the Shang rulers with soldiers and officers, as well as with workers for the many huge Shang construction projects.

Zhou Feudal Lords

Under the Zhou dynasty, many local leaders became **feudal** lords. The Zhou kings granted them power to govern states as part of Zhou territory. As in the Shang dynasty, the Zhou lords were required to provide the kings with soldiers and weapons. The status of a lord could be passed on to his sons. Becoming a lord involved ceremonies in which the king gave gifts to the lord. Unlike the Shang aristocrats, Zhou lords attended the king's court. They served the king as ministers—that is, officials of the government who managed part of the court's work.

Other members of the upper class—who were called the shih *(shee)*, or gentlemen—served the feudal lords. The shih included younger sons of lords, as well as some people who were not born into high status. Many of the shih had jobs under the ministers.

Qin Ranking System

In Qin **culture,** upper-class status mainly came from success in the army. The Qin status ranking system had 20 levels.

▲**Bronze vessel** inlaid with silver and glass from the Zhou dynasty. Powerful Zhou aristocrats could accumulate great wealth and, unlike most Chinese at that time, could afford such expensive luxuries.

THE PRIESTLY CLASSES

During the Shang **dynasty** (1766-1045 B.C.), the king was the most important religious leader. People believed the king's family had the closest connection to the highest god. There was also a class of people who helped the king in his religious role. Included in this class were **diviners**, invocators *(IHN vuh KAY tuhrz)*, and shamans *(SHAH muhnz)*.

Diviners

Using **rituals** to try to tell the future is called **divination** *(DIHV uh NAY shuhn)*. Diviners helped the king with rituals in which he tried to learn about future harvests or battles. In Shang times, the main way of telling the future was by using **oracle bones**.

◀ A divination, or prediction of the future, from the Shang dynasty written on a tortoise shell. Such divinations were read by members of the priestly class.

◀ A 4th century B.C. carved wooden figure with antlers made of dried lacquer. The Zhou dynasty figure probably represented a shaman; shamans often wore antlers while engaging in rituals performed as a means to communicate with the spirit world. The figure may have been placed at a tomb to serve as a guardian.

Invocators

Invocators were officials who also assisted with rituals. The invocator's job was to know the prayers and **invocations** (*IHN vuh KAY shuhnz*) from the past and to write new invocations when needed. Invocators also had to know the type of sacrifices necessary for certain rituals.

Shamans

Shamans were thought to act as intermediaries between the visible world and the invisible spirit world. They practiced magic to heal people and to control natural events such as weather. The shamans were the lowest members of the religious class.

Their jobs included performing dances to bring rain and guarding buried sacrifices. Shamans also went with lords or ladies to houses where people were mourning the dead. The **nobles** thought the shamans could keep evil spirits away. Ancient Chinese peasants also believed that the shamans could chase away evil spirits and help them talk to the dead.

THE WARRIOR CLASSES

Shang armies were often made up of as many as 3,000 to 5,000 men. While the armies included key members from the upper classes, most soldiers were men from the lower class. When a **noble** went to war, his followers went with him. Shang armies included both horse-drawn chariots and infantry, or foot soldiers. Only nobles had chariots.

The earliest-known Chinese chariots are from about 1200 B.C. During both the Zhou and Qin **dynasties**, chariots symbolized leadership.

The Warring States

By the time of the Warring States Period, war had become a big part of Chinese **culture,** and military officers even wrote books about warfare. One famous military officer, Sun Tzu *(soon tzoo)*, or Sunzi, wrote a book on military strategy entitled *The Art of War*, or *Ping-fa (pihng fah)* in Chinese.

Armies of the Warring States Period had huge numbers of infantry, who were mostly peasants. Nobles completely stopped taking part in combat during this time. Wars also became longer. During the earlier Spring and Autumn Period, a military campaign lasted no more than a season. During the Warring States Period, many campaigns lasted over a year.

▼ A **bronze** ax head from the Shang dynasty. Such axes were among the various weapons used by ancient Chinese warriors.

坑儒焚書 坑儒焚書 儒焚書

THE ART OF WAR

Sun Tzu's *The Art of War* includes instructions on how to plan for war, fight battles, use the terrain effectively, and make use of spies. The book states such military principles as:

• All war is based on deception.
• The best victories are those won without actually fighting.
• Countries do not benefit from prolonged warfare.

The Art of War is still studied by military strategists today. Many people also apply Sun Tzu's principles to such fields as business, diplomacy, politics, and sports.

The Qin Take Control

The Qin army—which eventually overthrew the Zhou dynasty—was said to have had 1 million soldiers, 1,000 chariots, and 10,000 horses. However, historians do not all agree on those figures. They do agree, however, that the number of people killed in battle increased greatly during the Warring States Period. This period set the stage for the Qin to take over and to found China's first unified **empire.**

▶ **Terra-cotta** warriors from the tomb of Shi Huangdi show the armor that was worn during the Qin dynasty.

THE ARTISAN, MERCHANT, AND FARMING CLASSES

During the Shang and Zhou **dynasties**, skilled workers, or **artisans**, specialized in crafting items in **bronze**. These people ranked below the leaders and **aristocrats** but above peasants. They used a method called **casting** to produce pots, **vessels** for wine and for **rituals,** weapons, and sculptures. Shang artisans also made pottery, **jade** carvings, and silk.

Late in the Zhou dynasty, Chinese artisans started working with iron. As with bronze, they made molds and cast the metal. They did not use iron for artworks, however; rather, it was cast into tools, such as knives.

Merchants

Trade increased greatly during the Zhou dynasty. The increase in trade led to the development of a class of merchants. Some merchants under the Zhou grew wealthy and became involved in politics.

▼ An artist's rendering of a busy marketplace in China during the Qin dynasty, a time when the emperor supported an increase in farming. A wide variety of produce and livestock, including pigs and geese, would have been available for sale.

▶ An animal-shaped wine vessel of bronze created by an artisan during the Shang dynasty.

Shang and Zhou Farmers

Farmers under the Shang dynasty were among the lower classes. In the northern part of China, farmers mainly grew a grain called millet *(MIHL iht)*. In the south near the Yangtze River, they grew rice. They also raised pigs, dogs, cattle, sheep, and horses. Farmers faced many problems. Pests and diseases could destroy their crops, leading to famine. Shang farmers believed that such disasters were caused by gods and spirits.

During the Zhou era, farmers had to turn over a certain amount of their crops to their lords, as a form of taxation. No one knows for sure how the crops were divided.

The Source of Wealth

Shi Huangdi, the Qin ruler, thought that farming was the source of wealth. He wanted as much land as possible to be planted with crops. Under his rule, each family was given a piece of land that could be worked by one adult man. This system also allowed him to keep track of men so he could draft soldiers and collect taxes.

SILK WEAVING

Silk fiber is a strong, shiny, threadlike substance that can be woven into cloth. It is extracted (taken) from the cocoons of caterpillars called silkworms, which feed on mulberry leaves. In ancient China, only wealthy people wore clothing made of silk, which is both cool in summer and warm in winter. Beginning in the Zhou era, silk was used as a form of money. People also wrote on it. Traditionally, women of the farming class produced silk. "Men plow and women weave," was a Zhou saying.

LAWS

Oracle bones and ancient books give us an idea of what laws were like in ancient China—and what happened to people who broke those laws.

Kings, Subjects, and Laws

During the Shang and Zhou **dynasties**, the king made all the laws. Kings probably claimed that the gods supported their laws. According to one ancient book, the Shang king Tang (*tahng*) said he would kill anyone who disobeyed him, along with the person's family. On the other hand, people of early China believed they had the right to topple cruel rulers. Tang did this to the Xia ruler, and the Zhou later did it to rulers of the Shang dynasty.

Inscriptions on oracle bones from the Shang dynasty mention lawsuits, judges, sentences, and legal rules. They suggest that there were rules about putting people in jail and about changing their punishments.

▲ A modern statue of the **legendary** Yellow Emperor, Huangdi, at what may be his birthplace in China's Henan **province.** Believed to have lived a thousand years before the beginning of the Shang dynasty and to have ruled for a hundred years, Huangdi is said to be the founder of Chinese civilization and to have given the first laws to the Chinese people.

Tough Punishments

Some punishments in early China could be very harsh. During the Zhou dynasty, people who broke the law could have a leg or an ear cut off. They also might have their noses sliced off or have an eye put out. Less harsh punishments included tattooing criminals' faces or their foreheads.

Statutes and Ordinances

Under the Qin dynasty, laws became highly rigid. As had been the case during earlier dynasties, punishments under the Qin emperor could include death, jail, or cutting off a part of the body of those who were found guilty.

The goal of many Qin laws was to prevent crime. Some Qin laws, however, were meant to shape society in positive ways. For example, the Qin had laws about farming that were meant to expand the economy. Farmers were forced to produce certain amounts of crops. Leaders issued written commands called lu *(loo)* and ling *(lihng)*. These documents told people what they must do and what would happen if they did not do it.

PUNISHMENT FOR ROBBERS

In 1975, 625 bamboo pieces with Qin laws written on them were found in a tomb at Hubei *(hoo bay)*. One law specified, "When five men jointly rob something worth one cash [a copper coin with a square hole in the center] or more, they should have their left foot cut off, be tattooed, and made convict laborers." These were criminals who were sentenced to "hard labor" (hard, enforced work with pay) as part of their punishment.

◀ A **bronze** "spade" coin from the Zhou dynasty. Theft, whether of money or of goods, was harshly punished in ancient China.

BELIEFS AND GODS

People of the early Chinese **dynasties** worshiped several gods. One, however, was higher than the others. During the Shang dynasty, the highest god was known as Di *(dee)*—the Lord—or Shangdi *(shahng dee)*—the Lord Above. During the Zhou dynasty, the highest god was known as Tian *(tyehn)*, or Heaven. The Zhou king was known as the Son of Heaven. The Chinese also worshiped Earth and **venerated** the spirits of their ancestors.

◀ A ritual **vessel** made during the Zhou dynasty is inscribed with a dedication to a deceased ancestor of the vessel's owner. For the Chinese, honoring ancestors was an important part of spiritual life. The decoration on the front of the vessel is in a style known as taotie *(tow tee eh)*.

DIVINING THE FUTURE

The late Zhou era is known as a time of new ideas. One major change was in **divination**. Instead of using **oracle bones**, people began using the *I Ching (ee jihng)*, or *The Book of Changes*. The *I Ching* contains diagrams that **diviners** still use to attempt to predict the future. The diviner tosses coins or sticks into the air. By comparing the pattern made by these objects, once they have fallen, to the meaning given for patterns shown in the book, people make predictions. In addition to its use for divination, the *I Ching* also has writings on **philosophy**.

Heaven and Earth

During the Shang era, people thought Di could affect military victories, the weather, and harvests. The Shang worshiped Di with **rituals** that included the sacrifice of animals and humans. The Shang believed that Di sometimes punished them by causing disasters or sending enemies to attack them.

By the Zhou era, only the king was allowed to worship Tian. The idea developed that each lord's territory had its own spirit related to Earth, which the Chinese called *she (shuh)*. Each lord worshiped at an altar representing the territory that he held and its spirit. The king, who ruled over both his own territory and over the **feudal** lords, worshiped both a *she* and Tian.

Honoring Worthy Ancestors

Along with praying to the gods, the early Chinese also honored their ancestors. A Zhou emperor, for example, would honor his most famous ancestor and the founder of the dynasty when praying to Tian. During the Zhou dynasty, people believed that the spirits of their ancestors could talk directly to Heaven for them.

Yin and Yang

During the late Zhou era, some thinkers began to see the world as guided by two opposite forces: **yin and yang**. They believed that these two forces balanced each other. The Chinese came to believe that the opposition between yin and yang was responsible for such movement as the turning from day to night and the changes in the seasons. During the short-lived Qin dynasty, religious practices followed those of the Zhou dynasty.

▲ The yin and yang symbol represents two opposite forces that balance each other. Ideas about yin and yang developed during the Zhou dynasty. The forces of yin and yang were thought to influence many aspects of life and nature and to be represented, for example, in the two-sided nature of such opposites as dark and light, weak and strong, cold and hot, and female and male.

CEREMONIES AND SACRIFICES

By the end of the Shang **dynasty**, the city of Yin was the center of government and palace life. Because the king, the main religious leader, lived at Yin, the city was the center of Shang religion. Under the modern Chinese city of Anyang, **archaeologists** have discovered more than a dozen foundations of buildings from the ancient city of Yin. They believe these buildings were temples. One of the structures is thought to have been an altar for sacrifices.

▼ Majestic Tai Shan mountain, in present-day Shandong **province,** was the site of fengchan ceremonies, which were performed by ancient Chinese kings and emperors when they had completed a great accomplishment.

Spirits and Sacrifices

Among the most important Shang ceremonies were those designed for the veneration of ancestors. During the Shang dynasty, people used stone tablets in temples to represent their ancestors. They believed that the spirits of the ancestors returned to the tablet for the veneration ceremonies. Archaeologists have never found an example of these tablets but know about them from descriptions on **oracle bones**.

Ceremonies carried out to **venerate** ancestors centered on sacrifices. People sacrificed grain, ale (a type of beer), cattle, dogs, sheep—even humans. The Shang ceremonies were bloody, fiery, and involved alcohol. The people probably believed that their all-powerful ancestors enjoyed the bloodshed—animal and human—as well as the smell of food.

◄ The skeletal remains of humans sacrificed at a Shang burial site in present-day Henan province. Burial ceremonies for Shang kings generally included human sacrifices, sometimes of large numbers of people.

The people of the Shang dynasty believed that these ceremonies would bring them rain, good harvests, children, and success in war and ward off evil spirits. During the Shang dynasty, these **rituals** were performed quite regularly. The highly regular cycle of veneration rituals helped archaeologists figure out the Shang calendar, which had six 10-day "weeks" that made up a 60-day cycle.

Fengchan

Kings performed the fengchan *(fuhng chahn)* ceremony when they had accomplished something great. Fengchan involved piling rocks on top of a mountain to bring humans closer to Heaven. Many fengchans were performed at Tai Shan *(ty shahn)*, a holy mountain. Shi Huangdi, the founder of the Qin dynasty and first emperor of China, is said to have performed fengchan at Tai Shan to mark the founding of his **empire**.

ARCHAEOLOGICAL EVIDENCE OF HUMAN SACRIFICE

Archaeologists **excavating** Yin have found that the burial ceremonies for Shang kings and **nobles** included many human sacrifices. Some of the victims are thought to have been servants or relatives of the dead person, and these victims did not have their bodies mutilated. Other sacrifice victims had their heads cut off, or even had their bodies cut in half at the waist. These victims, located farther away from the center of the tomb, are thought to be prisoners captured in wars.

Scientists have found far fewer human sacrifices in the tombs of the later Zhou dynasty kings.

Settlements

Very little is left of ancient Chinese settlements. The buildings are long gone; all that remains are some building foundations. Nevertheless, **archaeologists** have learned a lot about Shang cities from the remnants of the capital, Yin, and an earlier Shang capital, Zhengzhou *(juhng joh)*.

A City Wall

A huge wall, 4 miles (7 kilometers) around, surrounded Zhengzhou. At its base, the wall was about 105 feet (32 meters) thick. The highest part of the wall still remaining is 16 feet (5 meters) tall. It is made of rammed earth. Rammed-earth walls are made of layers of soil pressed or pounded together between two boards. After one layer is complete, the boards are moved, and the next layer is built on top of it. These walls are very durable.

Foundations

About 1,600 feet (500 meters) from the huge wall in Zhengzhou, archaeologists found more than 20 rammed-earth building foundations. Scientists believe that the same people who built the wall probably built these foundations. Nearby, archaeologists found workshops where **artisans** made items of **bronze**, pottery, and bone. Archaeologists also found graveyards. Their most shocking discovery was an ancient garbage dump that contained more than 100 skulls of young men. Some of the skulls had been sawn open at the brow. Archaeologists do not know why this was done.

Yin

Archaeologists think Yin was the last Shang capital. All that is left of this once-great city are 50 rammed-earth foundations. Most of these

The Palaces of Xianyang

According to both *The Historical Records*, or *Shi Ji*, and the finds of archaeologists, Xianyang, the Qin capital, contained grand palaces. Long corridors connected great halls. Huge roofs on the main buildings seemed to float above the people below. Decorations, furniture, food, chariots, and guards were all arranged to show the power and glory of Shi Huangdi. In several Xianyang buildings, archaeologists have found pieces of colorful paintings of people, horses and carriages, plants, and various animals.

▲ A rammed-earth building foundation at the ancient Shang capital Yin. Within the foundation walls, archaeologists have uncovered Shang dynasty **artifacts** made of bronze, pottery, and bone.

foundations range from 66 to 164 feet (20 to 50 meters) long. The longest foundation is 279 feet (85 meters). The site contains dwellings for workers, bronze workshops, and graveyards. Of more importance scientifically, it also contains 13 royal tombs, a great number of **oracle bones**, and evidence of sacrifices.

▲ A **terra-cotta** model of a walled farm. Such farms were common in the Zhou and Qin dynasties. The building in the center is the main dwelling.

Zhou Cities

Zhou cities also had rammed-earth foundations and surrounding walls. Archaeologists face a big problem in learning about Zhou settlements because sites of archaeological interest are often buried under existing towns and cities.

Important remains of Zhou cities include Wangcheng *(wohng cheeung)*, a site in present-day Xiaotun *(shyow toon)*. Wangcheng dates from the Spring and Autumn Period. The city center of Wangcheng was surrounded by a square of rammed-earth walls.

Qufu *(choo foo)* was another significant Zhou settlement. According to **legend**, Confucius *(kuhn FYOO shuhs)* was born in the city of Qufu, in the state of Lu *(loo)*. Confucius, who lived from about 551 B.C. to around 479 B.C., was the most influential and respected **philosopher** *(fuh LOS uh fuhr)* in Chinese history.

TOMBS

uch of our knowledge of China's early dynasties comes from objects found in tombs.

All Tombs Are Not Created Equal

The manner in which a body was buried in Shang times revealed a lot about that person's social status. Members of the highest class were buried in huge tombs. Their tombs were up to 40 feet (12 meters) deep and contained wooden burial chambers. Building these tombs required thousands of workers.

▼ Bones and buried **artifacts** found in the tomb of Lady Fu Hao, the wife of a Shang king, at Zhengzhou. The bones of sacrifice victims and valuable objects, known as grave goods, were often buried in the tombs of persons of high status during the Shang dynasty.

THE TOMB OF THE FIRST EMPEROR

At least one famous ancient Chinese coffin has never been opened. For more than 2,000 years, people have known that the burial place of Qin Emperor Shi Huangdi is at Xi'an. Pits containing thousands of life-sized **terra-cotta** statues were found at his burial site, and **archaeologists** have worked for years to **excavate** these pits (see pages 38-39). The actual burial chamber of the emperor has never been excavated, however. Ancient historians claimed that the chamber was a marvel. Some stated that the body of Shi Huangdi was surrounded by a huge model representation of his realm that included constellations painted on the ceiling and running rivers made up of mercury. It may be that the tales about the chamber were true. When archaeologists tested the ground surrounding the chamber in modern times, they found unusually high levels of mercury.

▲ A ting tripod, found in a Shang tomb, is decorated with dragon figures. A ting is a vessel in which food was placed as a ritual offering to ancestors.

Family members and servants of very high status people were sometimes killed—sacrificed—and buried in the tomb of the high-status person. The ancient Chinese believed that sacrificial victims would follow and continue to serve the person being buried in the afterlife. Tombs such as these were only for the very wealthy. Members of the middle classes were buried in pits. The bodies of the lowest classes were thrown into garbage dumps or into unused wells.

Well Equipped . . . to Die

When wealthier people died and were buried in ancient China, they were sent to the next world with **grave goods.** These are items placed in a tomb to indicate a person's status and to ensure that the dead person has the things he or she will need in the afterlife. These grave goods included personal possessions of the dead, containers of food, **vessels** made of **bronze**, hairpins, weapons, **oracle bones**, and jewelry. Sometimes, living creatures would be sent with the deceased, as well. Besides family members and servants, horses and dogs were sacrificed and buried in the tombs of **nobles**. The hope was to provide the dead with all they would need in the spirit world.

Tomb Variations

Early tombs of the Zhou dynasty, which were reserved for the upper classes, were built like Shang tombs, with deep pits and ramps. Many of these tombs contained grave goods.

The bronze objects in these tombs—including bells, **ritual** bronzes, and **tings** (tihngz), a type of pot standing on three legs—helped indicate the status of the person buried there. People with the highest status were buried with nine ting tripods. People of somewhat lower status had fewer tings. Most Zhou tombs, however, had no bronzes of any kind in them.

Another sign of status was burying a body in two coffins, one nested inside the other. These nested coffins were decorated with bronze ornaments and **lacquerware.**

ART AND SCULPTURE

Ancient China's most important artworks are **bronzes**. During the Shang **dynasty** and most of the Zhou dynasty, **artisans** crafted bronze objects of extraordinary quality and artistry. The size of some of the bronze **artifacts** remaining from Shang and Zhou times has surprised—and amazed—**archaeologists**. One Shang bronze **vessel**, the Simuwu *(soo moo woo)* tetrapod (a four-footed vessel), weighs 1,925 pounds (875 kilograms). Many of these vessels were used for **rituals**.

Shang and Zhou Bronzes

Max Loehr (*lohr*), a famous art historian who lived from 1903-1988, was a widely recognized expert on Shang dynasty bronzes. Loehr found that Shang bronzes came in five styles. Eventually, he was able to date bronzes to earlier or later times in the Shang dynasty based upon the style of an object's decoration. Common features found on all five styles of Shang bronzes were lined designs and taotie **motifs**, or repeated designs. Taotie is a mysterious animal-face image common on Shang bronzes. Some see taotie as a monster, while others see it as a dragon.

▼ A lacquerware bowl made during the Qin dynasty is decorated with a design of fish and a phoenix.

During the Zhou dynasty, artisans made many new and different types of bronze vessels. The decorations on these vessels were more detailed than those on Shang bronzes. Zhou bronzes also featured motifs not seen on Shang bronzes. For example, pictures of birds were common. Zhou bronzes also sometimes featured inscriptions that identified to whom they belonged. Owning a big collection of bronzes was a sign of status in Zhou society. Qin bronzes were much like the bronzes of the Zhou dynasty. This dynasty lasted for too short a time for the art to develop its own style.

▲ A carved jade elephant from the Shang dynasty.

Pottery

People of the Shang, Zhou, and Qin dynasties also made pottery. White pottery with carved designs was popular.

Lacquerware

The art of **lacquerware** developed in China as early as 300 B.C. Lacquerware is made by coating a base, usually a wooden form, with many layers of varnish, which the Chinese made from a tree sap.

Jade

The carving of **jade** was another common art form in ancient China. Some jade carvings were used in rituals. Small cicada *(suh KAY duh)* insect figures carved of jade were often placed in the mouths of the dead before burial. The cicada is a popular symbol of good fortune in China. Some experts believe that these jade pieces were meant to contain the soul of the dead to preserve it for the difficult journey from this life to the afterlife. Other experts speculate that the ancient Chinese believed that the jade pieces guaranteed the deceased a long and good existence in the afterlife.

RITUAL BRONZES

Most of the bronze vessels created in ancient China related in some way to food or drink. Food was central to worship in Chinese **culture.** Chinese worship centered on the ancestors of the family. Ancestors could intervene in this world to help or hinder the living. Food offerings were important in burial rites. After burial, food offerings continued to be the main way the ancient Chinese **venerated** dead ancestors.

THE TERRA-COTTA ARMY

In 221 B.C., Shi Huangdi, the founder of the Qin **dynasty**, became the first emperor of all of China. His power was immense. **Archaeologists** discovered just how immense in the 1970's.

Discovery of the Terra-Cotta Army

In 1974, farmers digging a well in Shanxi **province** found some pieces of **terra cotta**. Archaeologists examined the fragments and searched the area. They soon realized that the pieces were from the huge burial site of Shi Huangdi. Archaeologists located this site on the bank of the Wei *(way)* River in Xi'an.

The big surprise came when archaeologists searched the area around the tomb. About 1,640 yards (1,500 meters) from the tomb, they found three large pits. In them were thousands of life-sized terra-cotta statues of soldiers. It was an entire army, set up to protect the emperor's tomb and the emperor in the afterlife. The largest pit holds more than 6,000 statues of soldiers, including archers, foot soldiers, and charioteers. The second-largest pit also has terra-cotta soldiers and horses and nearly 100 wooden chariots. The smallest pit is thought to have represented army headquarters. It features a horse-drawn carriage escorted by a small group of foot soldiers.

▼ The so-called terra-cotta army consists of thousands of sculptures of soldiers found in pits near the tomb of Shi Huangdi. The pits in which the huge army stands are now enclosed under a roof for protection.

▲ The soldiers in the terra-cotta army have different facial features, hairstyles, and hats, and the statues are different heights. An "army" of craftsmen must have been needed to create these thousands of statues.

A Factory for Figures

The terra-cotta army was a huge project and required tremendous organization. Workers were assigned to any of several different workshops. The process for making the soldiers probably varied slightly from workshop to workshop. The figures were built from the bottom up. For the legs, artisans made models of solid clay. They joined each torso, made of coils of clay, to the lower part of the body. Heads were made from one or two molds, with hairdos and caps added separately. Artisans then painted each figure realistically.

No one knows how many terra-cotta figures remain buried. In 1999, archaeologists discovered a pit of figures of acrobats and artists. A couple of years later, they found terra-cotta birds and musicians. So far, more than 8,000 terra-cotta figures have been uncovered.

Making the Terra-Cotta Army

No two terra-cotta soldiers are alike. Their heights vary from 5 feet 8 inches (1.7 meters) to 6 feet 6 inches (2 meters). Each soldier was modeled with a different face. To produce such a huge number of different statues, **artisans** had to make separate heads, arms, torsos, and legs. They then put the pieces together. The soldier's equipment was the finishing touch. The terra-cotta soldiers were armed with real swords, spears, and bows. The weapons were stolen after the figures were created. At one time, the figures were painted in bright colors, but today only traces of that paint remain on some of the figures.

PHILOSOPHY

Confucius and other famous and influential **philosophers** lived during the time of the ancient Chinese **dynasties.**

Confucius

Confucius is China's most famous and influential philosopher. His goal was to teach people how to improve their behavior. He lived in a period of political disorder late in the Zhou era. Confucius taught that political disagreement would end if everyone followed a code of behavior set during the early Zhou dynasty—a code that dated to 600 years before Confucius's own birth.

The teachings of Confucius were strikingly simple. He believed everyone had a clear role in life. He arranged people in roles ranked from highest to lowest—he did not consider people to be equal. Each person had to figure out what his or her role was—father, ruler, son, husband, wife, farmer, **artisan**, etc. The instructions in the books handed down explain how a person should fulfill his or her role. If someone is a father or a son, for example, there are specific ways to fulfill that role to bring peace, harmony, and contentment. According to Confucius, when a person achieved harmony and contentment, others would try to pattern themselves on that person. Confucius believed that rulers and officials, as well as individuals, had a great responsibility to make this system work.

Confucius's followers gathered his ideas into a book entitled *The Analects.* Two of his students—Mencius *(MEN she ahs),* who lived c. 370 B.C. to 300 B.C., and Xunzi *(shyoon dzuh),* who lived c. 310 B.C. to 220 B.C.—also became important philosophers.

Laozi and Daoism

Another ancient Chinese **philosophy**, Taoism *(TOW ihz uhm),* which is also spelled Daoism *(DOW ihz uhm),* differed from Confucianism. Followers of Taoism believed

▲ A portrait of the great Chinese philosopher Confucius, who lived during the Zhou dynasty, is engraved on a pillar of stone, or stele *(STEE lee).* The engraving was created during the Tang dynasty (A.D. 618-907).

▲ A giant statue of Laozi, who is credited as being the founder of the beliefs known as Taoism, was carved during the Song *(soong)* dynasty (A.D. 960-1279). It is located in Quanzhou *(chwen joh)*, in present-day Fujian *(foo zhen)* **province**.

people should live in harmony with nature and avoid doing harm to others. One of the important books in Taoism is the *Tao Te Ching (dow duh jihng)*, which translates to *The Classic of the Way and the Virtue.* The word *tao* means *the road* or *the way.* The book is usually credited to Laozi *(low tzuh)*, also spelled Lao Tzu. Some historians, however, believe that there was no one person named Laozi and that the *Tao Te Ching* was the combined work of many authors. The *Tao Te Ching* was created around the 200's B.C.

Qin Legalism

As the state of Qin gained power, its leaders followed a philosophy called legalism. Legalism held that it was important for leaders to make firm laws. With firm laws and harsh punishments, they believed, a state could become strong and rich—and more powerful than other states.

TECHNOLOGY

The technologies developed during the Shang, Zhou, and Qin **dynasties** were among their great triumphs. We may take these technologies for granted today. Thousands of years ago, however, they were among the most advanced on Earth.

Metalworking

The early Chinese peoples already knew how to work **bronze** well before the Shang era, making such simple items as bracelets, knives, mirrors, and needles. Shang **artisans**, however, became highly skilled at **casting** bronze. To cast metal, the Shang carved a model of the object they wanted to make. They then baked clay around the model. The clay formed a mold for the object they wanted to make. They poured molten (melted) bronze into the mold and cast an object of bronze. **Archaeologists** have found such Shang casted bronze products as tools, cups, vases, cooking pots, and musical instruments.

By about the 700's B.C.—during the Zhou dynasty— the ancient Chinese also began to work iron. Their iron products included a variety of weapons and farm tools.

▲ A mold, which dates from the Zhou dynasty, allowed ancient Chinese metalworkers to cast two sickle (curved) blades at one time. Chinese artisans became skilled at casting, or using molds to create metal objects, during the Shang dynasty.

ANOTHER TECHNOLOGICAL ADVANCEMENT

The Qin dynasty was one of the first governments to set exact amounts for weights and measures. The government forced people to use only these units. Official Qin measuring tools had an inscription on them:

"In the 26th year, the emperor completely unified the lords of the **empire**. The common people were at ease. And he was designated as Huangdi, or sovereign emperor. He issued an edict . . . 'Standardized measurements. When they are not uniform or are in doubt, make them clear and make them uniform'."

Other Technologies

During the Warring States Period, soldiers began using the **crossbow**, which included a bronze trigger. This new weapon allowed soldiers to shoot farther than archers could with regular bows. Sometimes, several crossbows were mounted on a carriage and set up to be fired at the same time. Armor was another new technology first used by soldiers during the Warring States Period. Most of it was made of leather pieces tied together, though some iron armor and helmets have been found.

During the same era, Ximen Bao *(shee muhn bow)*, an official in the state of Wei, led the building of a system of canals for irrigation. This made it possible to farm land where crops had not grown before. Other irrigation projects began during the Qin dynasty (221-206 B.C.).

▲ A bronze **vessel,** dating from the Shang dynasty, was cast from a mold, a new technology developed during that time. Before the casting of metal was developed, artisans used bronze for such simple items as knives and needles.

FAMILY LIFE

In ancient China, fathers had total control over the lives of their children. They made decisions about their children's education and future work. They could also punish their children. Some historians believe that during the early days of ancient China, fathers could even put their children to death.

Eternal Respect

Filial piety *(FIHL ee uhl PY uh tee)* was crucial. Filial piety was more than respect. It was a duty owed to one's parents from whom one had received life and to whom one owed everything. In ancient China, disobeying one's parents or harming them in any way, even accidentally, was a major crime, often punished by death. Some historians think filial piety in ancient China eventually led to ancestor worship.

Marriage

Men ruled their children, but they probably did not rule their wives; that role was assumed by a husband's mother, a wife's mother-in-law. Girls married at about 16 years old. Their main goal was to have sons and raise families. Sons increased the family's standing in the community.

Some wealthy men had more than one wife. One wife was the main wife, and the others were ranked below her. No matter which mother a child was born to, however, all of a man's children were considered equal.

▶ A **jade** ancestor tablet from the Shang **dynasty**. Information written on such tablets included the name of the person who had died and that person's birth and death dates, as well as the name of the son or other relative who had the tablet created. After the funeral ceremony, the tablet was placed in a shrine at the family's home.

Family Names

Ancient China was one of the first **cultures** in which people had family names, or surnames. Most of these names derived from clans—that is, a group of families that believed themselves to be descended from a common ancestor. No one knows what the original meanings of these early Chinese surnames would have been. In ancient China, men and women with the same surname were thought to be related and could not marry.

▼ Stone figures from the 200's B.C. of a woman kneeling in respect before a man, possibly a husband, whose face has been tattooed.

THE ZHOU WEDDING CEREMONY

Some important people in ancient China believed in marriage to only one person at a time, or monogamy *(muh NOG uh mee)*. The brother of one of the first Zhou kings invented a marriage ceremony to encourage monogamy. The ceremony had six main steps, which had to be performed at sunrise or sunset. It was believed that sunrise and sunset were the times when **yin and yang** met. In addition, the ideas "man" and "woman" were also associated with yin and yang, so sunrise and sunset were fitting times for them to meet.

At each of the six stages, the groom's family gave the bride's family a live, wild goose. The goose—which chooses one mate for life—symbolizes monogamy.

SHELTER

In ancient China, the type of house people lived in depended on their class.

Upper-Class Palaces

Rulers and other **nobles** lived in large, aboveground buildings. The buildings were rectangular, with rammed-earth foundations. Many palaces consisted of buildings around a courtyard. The courtyard had a central gate; there was often a second courtyard behind the first, connected with another gate. The most important rooms were located at the back of a courtyard and in the rear courtyards. These rooms would have had the highest and most elaborate tiled roofs.

◀ A **terra-cotta** model of a house, similar to houses of the Zhou and Qin dynasties. Such model houses are often found in tombs from these dynasties and were made to accompany the house's owner to the afterworld. The central tower, or cupola (*KYOO puh luh*), probably served as a chimney. The tile roof and porch suggest that the house upon which this was modeled would have been owned by a wealthy person.

Archaeologists examine the foundations of ancient Chinese buildings to try to understand what a house would have been like. They imagine that one Zhou palace in Shanxi **province** had a huge hall at the center and many rooms surrounding courtyards. By looking at foundations, they can also get an idea of a building's height. Taller palaces were built on thicker foundations.

Houses

During the Shang era, most **artisans** lived in aboveground houses with rammed-earth walls. These houses had two rooms and often a window. A woven lattice (strips of crossed wood) cover on these windows let in some light and kept out animals.

Medium-sized houses from the Qin era may have had more than one level and rooms built around a courtyard. They had wood frames, thatched (straw) or tiled roofs, and walls made of rammed-earth, brick, or mud. One way we know about these buildings is from models left in tombs.

▶ Bronze lamp from the Zhou **dynasty** used as a source of light in an upper-class household. The bowl possibly held burning oil or coal.

PEASANT DWELLINGS

In addition to the palace foundations and tombs at Yin, archaeologists found many pit houses. These houses were partially underground. Most of the people who lived in them were probably common people. However, archaeologists have found tools for working **bronze**, stone knives, and **jades** in some of these houses. These findings suggest that at least some artisans may also have lived in pit houses during the Shang era.

FOOD AND CLOTHING

Grains—including millet, rice, and wheat—were staple foods in ancient China. Vegetables included garlic, leeks, onions, and turnips. The Chinese grew apricot, pear, and plum trees. People raised chickens, cows, dogs, deer, horses, pigs, and sheep for meat. In the fields and hills, they hunted wild boar, hare, and muntjac (*MUHNT jak*), a kind of small deer. Fish and shellfish were also eaten.

Seasonings and sauces were used to add flavor to meals. Food was prepared in many ways, including boiling, frying, roasting, drying, and pickling. Many dishes combined a variety of ingredients.

Pots for Food and Drink

Most of the ancient Chinese **bronzes** that are in museums were used for **rituals.** Ordinary people in ancient China used ceramic (fired-clay) items for household purposes. Wealthy people from the time, however, sometimes used bronze items for cooking. Two examples of ancient Chinese bronzes used for cooking are the **ting** and the yan (*yehn*). The ting is a pot, usually with three or four legs. A fire could be built under it. The yan is another type of pot. It is similar in shape to the ting, except that it has space in its legs for water and an inner rack. The yan was used for steaming food. The jue (*joo eh*) and the gu (*goo*) were types of **vessels** that were used for wine.

◀ A figure of a seated woman wearing a one-piece robe, or shenyi. The statue is one of many terra-cotta sculptures that was buried near the tomb of Shi Huangdi.

BIRDS, BEES, AND BEYOND

The ancient Chinese ate many types of birds, including quail, partridge, pheasant, sparrow, and curlew (*KUR loo*—a relative of the sandpiper). They also made meals from frogs, snails, and insects, including cicadas, moths, and bees.

Clothing

During the Shang **dynasty** (1766-1045 B.C.) and the Zhou dynasty (1045-256 B.C.), basic clothing included a yi *(yee)* and a shang *(shahng)*. The yi was a coat, and the shang was a skirt worn beneath the yi.

During the Shang era, yi had narrow sleeves and no buttons. They were tied at the waist with a sash. They were probably made of woven linen or silk. These garments were dyed in a wide variety of colors. By the Zhou era, sleeves of yi could be wide or narrow. Skirts could reach the floor or only to the knees. Some people added **jade** ornaments to their sashes.

During the Spring and Autumn Period and the Warring States Period, late in the Zhou dynasty, the shenyi *(shuhn yee)* became popular. The shenyi was a one-piece robe that was worn by both men and women of different classes.

Peasants would have worn simpler clothing, but their clothing was similar in style to that described above. Using clothing to indicate social rank was a later development in China.

▲ The remains of a jade necklace from the Shang dynasty.

EDUCATION

There were no schools in the Shang **dynasty**. Only people of the upper classes could read and write. Adults taught children, usually only boys, with informal lessons.

China's First Schools

Wen Wang *(wen wong)*, who became the first king of the Zhou dynasty, is said to have founded ancient China's first educational system. This system had primary schools for boys, who started at age 8. The pupils attended school until they were 15 years old. Good students could then go on to an advanced academy in the Zhou capital. The academy taught both these students and the sons of the upper class.

Confucius

The **philosopher** Confucius was said to be an excellent teacher. He taught many boys and young men and had hundreds of followers. He believed that most people could become good people and believed in the importance of tradition and **rituals**. Confucius wanted his students to be of strong moral character and to put their knowledge to work in government service. Students of Confucius spread his ideas. By the time of the Han dynasty (206 B.C. to A.D. 220)— immediately after the short-lived Qin dynasty—students studied Confucius in state schools.

▲ A contemporary Chinese boy works at developing the art of writing Chinese characters, a skill that takes a great deal of practice.

THE BURNING OF THE BOOKS

Many historians of ancient China believe that the Qin government burned books it did not want people to read. This is one of the reasons people criticize Shi Huangdi. A recent book by Mark Edward Lewis, a professor of Chinese **culture** at Stanford University in California, however, claims that this is not true. Lewis suggests that the forces of Xiang Yu *(shyahng yoo)*, the leader who overthrew the Qin dynasty, burned the books when they burned the Qin library.

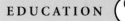

坑儒焚書

Qin Control

The Qin dynasty wanted complete control over society. Shi Huangdi did not want people to question his laws. One way he controlled people was by controlling education. He had commonly studied books, such as *The Book of Songs* and *The Book of Documents* (see pages 52 and 53), taken away from people and put into libraries. The Qin government then appointed special teachers who were the only ones allowed to study these texts. The goal of Qin education was to produce good government workers.

▲ A watercolor painting from the 1600's shows the burning of books and the execution of scholars that is supposed to have been carried out under Shi Huangdi. According to some historians, China's first emperor did not want people to question his laws and so controlled access to books and education.

LITERATURE

Several books from the Zhou **dynasty** have become classics of Chinese literature. People still read *The Analects* of Confucius and the *Tao Te Ching* and still turn to the *I Ching* for its **philosophy** or for **divination**. They read *The Book of Songs* and *The Book of Documents* to learn about Zhou history and tradition.

The Book of Songs

Written early in the Zhou dynasty, *The Book of Songs* contains 305 poems. About half of its contents are popular songs of ancient China. Love, work, marriage, and war are among their topics. The other half of the book tells of the greatness of early Zhou leaders or problems with later leaders. Life at the Zhou royal court, as well as the achievements of the royal family, are common themes. Confucius is said to have edited *The Book of Songs*.

▼ A portion of *The Analects* of Confucius. The manuscript, created during the Tang dynasty (A.D. 618–907), was discovered in 1967 in China's modern-day Xinjiang (*shihn jee ahng*) region.

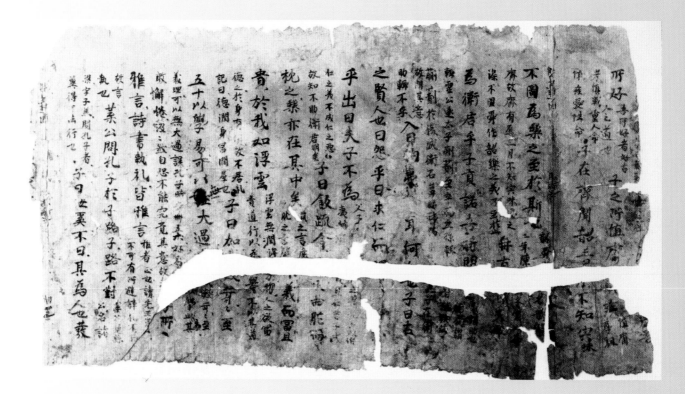

The Book of Documents

Another early Zhou-era book, *The Book of Documents*, concerns history and politics. It contains speeches and debates between early Zhou kings about different problems in politics. One topic is the Zhou conquest of the Shang and their reasons for it. The Zhou believed that the Shang dynasty lost the right to rule because its king had become corrupt and cruel. Some scholars believe that not all of the documents are authentic early Zhou texts. But even if some documents were written later, scholars agree that they still date from before the 1st century B.C.

The Historical Records

Also known as *Shi ji*, *The Historical Records* were largely written by Si Ma Qian (*sih mah chyen*), who lived from about 145 B.C. to 85 B.C. Si Ma Qian lived during the Han dynasty. *The Historical Records* covers a huge amount of history, including the Shang, Zhou, and Qin dynasties. It contains chronicles of historical events, treaties, and biographies. The biographies are the most famous and most consulted sections of this huge work. Si Ma Qian often described two individuals of widely different personalities and character in a single chapter.

▲ A watercolor painting from a later period depicts scribes making a copy of the *Tao Te Ching*, a collection of Taoist teachings from the 200's B.C., for presentation to the emperor.

MUSIC AND DANCE

Although some of the poems in *The Book of Songs* could probably be sung, no musical compositions from ancient China still exist. In spite of this, **archaeologists** are sure that music was an important part of life in ancient China. Kings and lords often had musicians and dancers in their courts. Songs from *The Book of Songs* were part of **rituals** for **venerating** ancestors.

Musical Instruments

Archaeologists have discovered many ancient Chinese musical instruments. At least 124 were uncovered in the tomb of a **nobleman** of Zeng *(tzuhng)*, located in the modern **province** of Hubei *(hoo bay)*. These included drums, flutes, zithers (a string instrument), and a 64-piece set of bells.

▼ Bronze bells from the Zhou **dynasty.** Bells were commonly used as musical instruments in ancient China.

抗儒焚書 抗儒焚書 抗儒焚書

BIANZHONG: THE BELLS OF ANCIENT CHINA

A 64-bell set found in a nobleman's tomb was mounted on a wooden frame. It is the most complete set of ancient Chinese bells ever found. The bells are of different sizes. Players struck them to create a tune. Together, the bells make up a musical instrument called a bianzhong *(bee uhn johng)*. Bell sets were hung, in order of size, from large wooden beams so they could be played.

Bells are excellent examples of ancient Chinese metalworking skills. Some bells required **artisans** to make up to 38 separate molded pieces. Certain bell sets have details of the ancient Chinese system of musical scales inscribed on them.

Dance

Not much is known about how the people of Shang, Zhou, and Qin times danced. Archaeologists have found evidence of dancing in ancient China on **artifacts**. Pictures of dancers decorate some **bronze** bowls from the Warring States Period (475-221 B.C.). In a tomb in Shandong province, archaeologists found a set of small statues that includes figures of dancers. They also believe that a dance step called the Pace of Yu was part of some good-luck rituals.

The Power of Music

Ancient Chinese **philosophers** believed music could have a strong effect on people. Confucius claimed that certain music could help people get along and that other music could make them think negative thoughts. The philosopher Xunzi encouraged leaders to use music to influence their people. He said that calm music could encourage harmony and that serious, harsh-sounding music could provoke people into obedience.

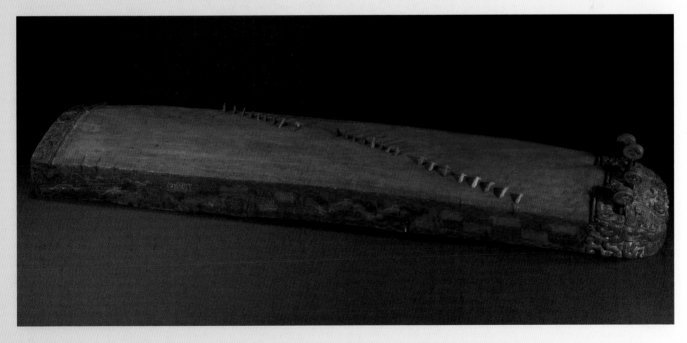

▲ An ancient Chinese stringed instrument called a qin typically had seven strings, usually made out of silk. Qin were often beautifully lacquered, as is this example made during the late Zhou dynasty.

DECLINE OF THREE DYNASTIES

Over time, all three **dynasties**—the Shang, the Zhou, and the Qin—fell. Both the Shang and the Qin dynasties ended when a weakened ruler was overthrown by a more powerful rival. The Zhou had a more gradual decline over a long period of infighting among local rulers during the time known as the Warring States Period.

Decline of the Shang

According to *The Historical Records*, the last Shang king, Di Xin *(dee shihn)*, was a brilliant and ferocious man. After taking the throne, he set out on military expeditions to prove his might. During his rule, he also became known for drinking too much alcohol, treating others cruelly, and demanding great luxury.

JIZI'S WORRIES ABOUT THE END OF THE SHANG DYNASTY

According to the historian Hanfeizi *(han fay tzuh)*, even a member of Di Xin's own family—Di Xin's uncle, Jizi *(tsee tzuh)*—worried about the effect Di Xin would have on the Shang dynasty:

"With ivory chopsticks and **jade** bowls, he will certainly not be content with coarse fare, rough clothing, or thatched dwellings [houses with straw roofs]. He will have garments of many layers of silk, high pavilions [tents], and spacious halls. And he will demand everything in similar measure; and the whole world may not be enough to gratify his wants. How much do I dread the end!"

▲ A war chariot and skeleton found at a royal tomb at the site of Yin, the Shang capital. The Shang dynasty fell when it was attacked and its last king overthrown by the Zhou.

Zhou leaders believed that only just and upright leaders such as themselves had the right to rule. In 1045 B.C., a huge Zhou army—45,000 soldiers and 300 chariots—attacked Di Xin's army and won a quick victory.

Decline of the Zhou

Zhou power declined gradually during the Spring and Autumn Period and the Warring States Period, which actually lasted for hundreds of years. As Zhou states competed for power, the authority of the Zhou dynasty slowly lessened and the **feudal** system died out. At the same time, people began to think of all the ancient Chinese states as one land. They considered the Zhou ruler as the king of "All-Under-Heaven." Even when the Zhou kings had no power, the idea of All-Under-Heaven remained important to the people.

A Fast Rise and Fall

Shi Huangdi, founder of the Qin dynasty, rose to power during the Warring States Period. He defeated and unified the warring states, ending Zhou rule. Shi Huangdi wanted complete control. He punished or murdered anyone who questioned the government and pressed hundreds of thousands of people into hard labor. He also did not allow people to keep their traditions. Shi Huangdi went too far with his harsh rule, and would-be assassins tried to kill him three different times. When a group of soldiers rebelled against the emperor's government, many people joined them. Nevertheless, he held onto power until his death in 210 B.C.

After Shi Huangdi's death, his dynasty fell into chaos, and members of the court began murdering other members. The Qin dynasty collapsed in 206 B.C., falling to the Han dynasty.

▼ A **terra-cotta** figure that guarded a tomb from the Han dynasty, which came to power in 206 B.C. The Qin dynasty fell to the Han just a few years after the death of Shi Huangdi.

LEGACY OF ANCIENT CHINA

▲ The Great Wall north of Beijing, capital of present-day China, is one of the world's great tourist attractions.

Like the Qin dynasty before it, the Han **dynasty** built a powerful central government to rule China as one nation. The idea of a single government ruling all of China is an important legacy of the Qin dynasty that continues to unite a large and very diverse nation.

Philosophy and Religion

The Analects and other classic Confucian texts profoundly influenced Chinese thought, family structure, and government for thousands of years. Communist leader Mao Zedong (1893-1976), who controlled China from 1949 until his death, attempted to replace traditional Chinese **philosophy** with Communist ideology. Confucius was out, replaced by Mao's "little red book" of slogans. This was especially true during the Cultural Revolution that began in 1966. Mao sought to eliminate much that was traditional or old in Chinese **culture** and create in its place a new revolutionary culture. The resulting upheaval in Chinese society unleashed widespread chaos, crippled the economy, and resulted in the deaths of tens of thousands, perhaps hundreds of thousands, of people. After Mao's death, the Cultural

▲ A bronze, animal-shaped **ting** dating from the Spring and Autumn Period. Artistic bronze objects are one of the lasting legacies of the Zhou dynasty.

ANCIENT CHINESE ART IN MUSEUMS
Visitors to major museums around the world can enjoy viewing and learning about objects from ancient China. The Smithsonian Institution, in Washington, D.C., features bronze **ritual vessels** from the Shang and Zhou dynasties. The British Museum, in London, has a collection of ancient Chinese jade objects that includes human and animal figures from Shang and Zhou times. In China, the galleries of the Shanghai Museum display ancient Chinese bronzes and sculptures, as well as examples of early Chinese writing and pottery.

Revolution was publicly criticized by national leaders, who held Mao responsible. Afterward, the Chinese reexamined and slowly embraced some of their traditions dating back to the dynasties of ancient China.

Today, teachers in some schools once again begin the day by having pupils read from *The Analects.* Many people in China once again follow Confucius's ideas about courtesy and respect for the old.

Tao Te Ching and *I Ching*

The Taoist belief in following the order of nature has influenced many parts of Chinese culture, including philosophy, literature, medicine, and art. The *Tao Te Ching* has been translated into many languages and remains a primary source for people who want to learn about Taoism. The *I Ching* has also had lasting influence far beyond China.

Tourism

The rich history and artistic achievements of ancient China's dynasties have made China one of the world's great centers of tourism. The **terra-cotta** army is one of China's most popular attractions. Visitors can see the figures just as they were buried by the first emperor more than 2,000 years ago.

People from around the world travel to China to see the Great Wall, to visit the Palace Museum in Beijing, and to tour the Yin ruins in Anyang. Among the museum's greatest treasures are the **bronzes** and **jade artifacts** from the Shang and Zhou dynasties. At the Yin ruins, visitors can see the tomb of Fu Hao, remnants of the city wall, and artifacts of a truly remarkable culture.

GLOSSARY

alliance A union formed by agreement, joining the interests of people or states.

archaeological site A place where remains of past human **cultures** are found.

archaeologist A scientist who studies the remains of past human **cultures.**

aristocrat A person of the aristocracy, or upper class.

artifact An object or the remains of an object, such as a tool, made by people in the past.

artisan A person skilled in some industry or trade.

bronze A metal made mostly of copper and tin.

casting A method of shaping an object by pouring a liquid—such as molten metal—into a mold and letting the liquid harden. Once the metal hardened, the mold was removed.

crossbow A weapon used for shooting arrows. It had a bow mounted horizontally across the end of a handle. To load the crossbow, the archer drew the bowstring back to a catch. To shoot, the archer pulled a trigger that released the string.

culture A society's arts, beliefs, customs, institutions, inventions, language, technology, and values.

divination Trying to learn about the future by magical or supernatural means.

diviner A person who tries to tell the future by magical or supernatural means.

dynasty Members of the same family who rule a place.

empire A group of nations or states under one ruler or government.

excavate To uncover or unearth by digging, especially used of **archaeological sites.**

feudal A type of government in which a king gives land to be ruled by lords, who are beneath the king in power and importance. The lords swear loyalty to the king and promise to give him military help and other services.

filial piety Love and respect for one's parents, elders, and ancestors.

grave goods Items buried with a dead person, often meant to help and aid the dead in the afterlife.

invocation A prayer or call to gods or ancestors for help.

Iron Age The period of history that began between 1500 and 1000 B.C. in Europe with the widespread use of iron for tools and weapons. This period in China began a little later, in about 700 B.C.

jade A hard, tough, and highly colored stone. Jade comes in a wide range of colors, including dark green, white, yellow, gray, red, and black.

lacquerware Objects made by coating an article, such as a box, dish, tray, or vase, with many layers of varnish. The varnish may be clear or colored, and it forms a durable, glossy, waterproof surface that can be painted, carved, or decorated in other ways.

legend A folk story, often set in the past, which may be based in truth, but which may also contain fictional or fantastic elements. Legends are similar to myths, but myths often are about such sacred topics as gods or the creation of the world.

motif A repeated or featured design.

noble or **nobleman** or **-woman** A person of high standing in his or her **culture.**

oracle bones Animal bones, or sometimes turtle shells, with markings or writing on them. These items were used in **rituals** of the ancient Chinese to ask questions of gods and ancestors.

philosopher A lover of wisdom; person who studies **philosophy**.

philosophy The study of human nature and such ideas as the meaning of life and the best way to live.

pictogram A picture symbol in certain writing systems that could be used to stand for an idea, a sound, or a name.

province A division of a country or **empire**.

ritual A solemn or important act or ceremony, often religious in nature.

terra cotta A type of baked clay used in many different ways. Terra cotta is often used in fine art—for example, vases, statues and statuettes, and decorations on buildings are sometimes made from terra cotta. It can also be used as a construction material.

ting A **bronze** bowl with three legs, used in offerings of food to ancestors in **rituals.**

venerate To regard with deep respect; to honor.

vessels Hollow containers.

yin and yang Two opposite forces that the Chinese believe balance each other in the universe. Yin represents heaven, among other things, and yang represents Earth.

ADDITIONAL RESOURCES

Books

Ancient China
by Tony Allan (Chelsea House, 2007)

Ancient China
by Jane Shuter (Heinemann Library, 2006)

The Ancient Chinese
by Virginia Schomp (Franklin Watts, 2004)

National Geographic Investigates Ancient China
by Jacqueline Ball and Richard Levey (National Geographic Children's Books, 2006)

Projects About Ancient China
by Ruth Bjorklund (Benchmark Books, 2006)

The Technology of Ancient China
by Robert Greenberger (Rosen Publishing, 2006)

Web Sites

http://china.mrdonn.org/index.html

http://historylink101.com/china/china_maps.htm

http://www.ancientchina.co.uk/menu.html

http://www.discoverychannel.co.uk/ancient_china/index.shtml

http://www.mrdowling.com/613chinesehistory.html

INDEX

Acknowledgments

AKG Images: 53 (Erich Lessing); **Alamy:** 26 (F. Jack Jackson), 32, 34 (China Images), 56 (DK); **The Art Archive:** 1, 28, 42, 43, 48, 59 (Genius of China Exhibition), 16 (British Library, London), 20, 54, 57 (Musée Guimet Paris/Gianni Dagli Orti), 22, 33, 45, 46 (Musée Cernuschi Paris/Gianni Dagli Orti), 25, 37 (Beijing Institute of Archaeology/Laurie Platt Winfrey), 27 (Jan Vinchon Numismatist Paris/Gianni Dagli Orti), 51 (Bibliothèque Nationale, Paris); **Bridgeman Art Library:** 17, 18 (Bibliothèque Nationale, Paris); **The British Museum:** 19; **Corbis:** 5 (Free Agents Limited), 6, 41 (Liu Liqun), 11, 36, 47, 49, 55 (Asian Art & Archaeology Inc.), 23 (Miguel Menéndez V./epa), 30 (Demetrio Carrasco/JAI), 31 (Lowell Georgia), 38 (Jose Fuste Raga), 39 (Xiaoyang Liu), 50 (Keren Su), 52 (Bettmann), 58 (Chen Xiaodong/Xinhua Press); **Freer Gallery of Art, Smithsonian Institution, Washington, D.C.:** 44 (Gift of Charles Lang Freer); **Shutterstock:** 29 (Thorsten Rust); **Topfoto:** 21 (The British Museum/HIP); **Werner Forman Archive:** 8 (The Palace Museum, Beijing), 9 (British Library, London), 13, 14, 15 (no photographer credited), 35 (The National Gallery, Prague), 40 (Shaanxi Provincial Museum, Xian).

Cover image: **Bridgeman Art Library** (Bibliothèque Nationale, Paris)
Back cover image: **Shutterstock** (Joop Snijder, Jr.)